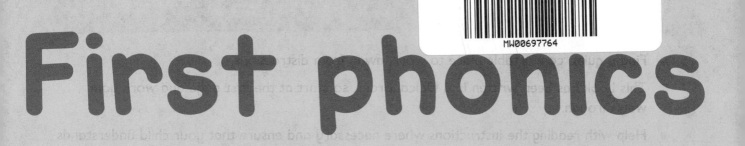

First phonics

This book belongs to

....

Colour the star when
you complete a page.
See how far you've come!

4 5 6 7 8

9 10 11 12 13

14 15 16 17 18

19 20 21 22 23

Author: Carol Medcalf

How to use this book

- Find a quiet, comfortable place to work, away from distractions.

- This book has been written in a logical order, so start at the first page and work your way through.

- Help with reading the instructions where necessary and ensure that your child understands what to do.

- This book is a gentle introduction to 26 of the 44 sounds of the English language. Working through the book, your child will start to realise that words are made up of small separate sounds. These individual sounds are called phonemes; bus, for example, is made up of three phonemes: b-u-s. Encourage your child to sound out each letter sound before they attempt to sound-blend the whole word. For example, say 'kuh-a-tuh' and then read 'cat'.

- If an activity is too difficult for your child then do more of our suggested practical activities (see Activity note) and return to the page when you know that they're likely to achieve it.

- Always end each activity before your child gets tired so that they will be eager to return next time.

- Help and encourage your child to check their own answers as they complete each activity.

- Let your child return to their favourite pages once they have been completed. Talk about the activities they enjoyed and what they have learnt.

Special features of this book:

- **Progress chart:** when your child has completed a page, ask them to colour in the relevant star on the first page of the book. This will enable you to keep track of progress through the activities and help to motivate your child.

- **Activity note:** situated at the bottom of every left-hand page, this suggests further activities and encourages discussion about what your child has learnt.

- **Certificate:** the certificate on page 24 should be used to reward your child for their effort and achievement. Remember to give them plenty of praise and encouragement, regardless of how they do.

Published by Collins
An imprint of HarperCollinsPublishers Ltd
The News Building
1 London Bridge Street
London SE1 9GF

HarperCollinsPublishers
Macken House, 39/40 Mayor Street Upper,
Dublin 1, D01 C9W8, Ireland

Browse the complete Collins catalogue at collins.co.uk

First published 2015
This edition © HarperCollinsPublishers Ltd 2022

24
ISBN 978-0-00-815163-8

The author asserts the moral right to be identified as the author of this work.

Written by Carol Medcalf
Page layout by Contentra Technologies Ltd
Illustrations by Jenny Tulip and Contentra Technologies Ltd
Cover design by Sarah Duxbury and Amparo Barrera
All images ©Shutterstock.com and ©HarperCollinsPublishers
Project managed by Sonia Dawkins and Tracey Cowell
Printed and bound in the United Kingdom

FSC™ C007454
MIX
Paper | Supporting responsible forestry
www.fsc.org

Contents

Phonic sounds s and a

- Say the **s** sound. Draw a line from the letter **s** to each picture that starts with that sound.

- Say the **a** sound. Draw a line from the letter **a** to each picture that starts with that sound.

Emphasise the first sounds in words. Say: 'ttttt-train, sssss-snake, rrrrr-red'.

Phonic sounds t and p

● Say the **t** sound. Draw a line from the letter **t** to each picture that starts with that sound.

● Say the **p** sound. Draw a line from the letter **p** to each picture that starts with that sound.

Phonic sounds i and n

- Say the **i** sound. (Circle) each picture that starts with the **i** sound.

- Say the **n** sound. Colour each picture that starts with the **n** sound.

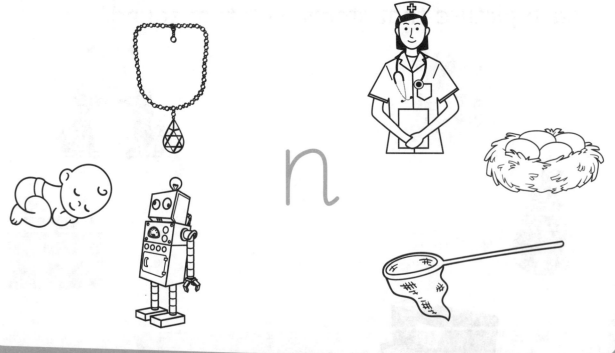

Practice time!

Now you have learnt the sounds **s**, **a**, **t**, **p**, **i** and **n**.

● Say the word for each picture. Draw a (circle) round the letter sound it starts with.

(s) t p a

t p a n

n i t s

a p n i

p s i t

i n s a

Phonic sounds m and d

- Say the **m** sound. Circle the pictures that do **not** start with the **m** sound.

- Say the **d** sound. Colour the pictures that do **not** start with the **d** sound.

When speaking to your child every day, emphasise individual letter sounds in three-letter words (such as 'c-a-t' or 'r-u-n') to help them practise their sound-blending skills. 'Look at the ç ą ţ' or 'Can you ŗ ų ṇ?' Always use clear phonetic sounds.

Phonic sounds g and o

- Say the **g** sound. Draw a line from the letter **g** to each picture that starts with that sound.

- Say the **o** sound. Draw a line from the letter **o** to each picture that starts with that sound.

Phonic sounds c and k

● Say the **c** sound. Draw a line from the letter **c** to each picture that starts with that sound.

● Say the **k** sound. Draw a line from the letter **k** to each picture that starts with that sound.

Children are, in general, taught to write a 'curly k' (k) but some schools will teach children to write a 'straight k' (k). From an early age, they will be shown both forms of the letter k so that they can recognise them.

Practice time!

Now you have learnt the sounds **m**, **d**, **g**, **o**, **c** and **k**.

- Circle the pictures that start with the letter sound shown at the beginning of each row.

m

d

g

o

c

pk

Phonic sounds e and u

● Colour the pictures that start with the letter sound shown at the beginning of each row.

e

u

e

u

Phonic sounds r and h

● (Circle) the pictures that start with the letter sound shown at the beginning of each row.

Phonic sounds b and f

● Say the **b** sound. Draw a line from the letter **b** to each picture that starts with that sound.

● Say the **f** sound. Draw a line from the letter **f** to each picture that starts with that sound.

There may be words that your child has never heard before such as 'fire', 'fan' or 'quail' (the bird picture used on page 18). A great way to extend language and learning is to look the item up, talk to them about it and include it in conversations.

Practice time!

Now you have learnt the sounds **e**, **u**, **r**, **h**, **b** and **f**.

● Say the word for each picture. Circle the letter sound it starts with.

d

e

u

o

r

c

h

s

t

b

k

f

Phonic sounds l and j

- Say the **l** sound. (Circle) each picture that starts with the **l** sound.

- Say the **j** sound. Colour each picture that starts with the **j** sound.

Make shakers together with your child using old plastic pots with lids. Fill the pots with things such as pebbles, sand, rice and dried pasta. Shake them and guess what is inside; this really helps with listening skills and with hearing sounds in words and sound-blending.

Phonic sounds v, w and x

- Circle the pictures that start with the letter sound shown at the beginning of each row.

v

w

x

- Draw lines to match the letter sounds to the pictures.

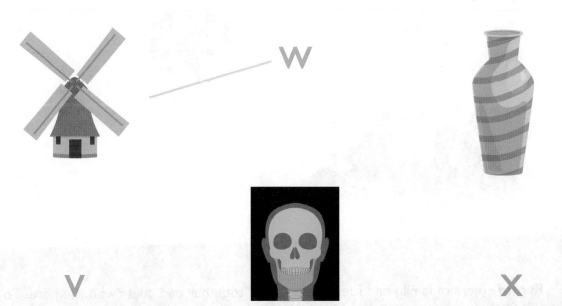

W

v   X

Phonic sounds y, z and qu

- (Circle) the pictures that start with the letter sound shown at the beginning of each row.

- Draw lines to match the letter sounds to the pictures.

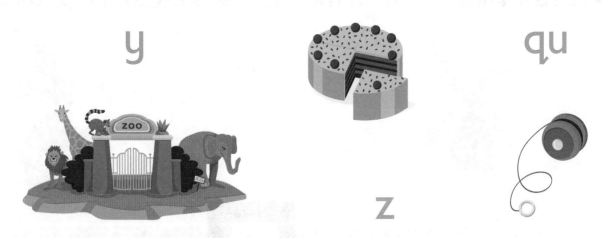

Practice time!

Now you have learnt the sounds **l, j, v, w, x, y, z** and **qu**.

- Circle the pictures that start with the letter sound shown at the beginning of each row.

l

j

v

w

x

y

z

qu

Alphabet sounds

● Draw lines to match the letter sounds to the pictures.

k

h

j

l

i

m

More alphabet sounds

● Draw lines to match the letter sounds to the pictures.

p

r

n

s

o

q

When out walking, play the silence game. Be very quiet and listen, then, after a while, discuss all the sounds you heard.

22

x

t

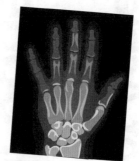

v

z

y

w u

Collins Easy Learning

Certificate of Achievement

Well done!

This certificate is awarded to ....

for successfully completing ....

Age ....

Date ....

Signed ....